PIANO / VOCAL / GUITAR

OVER THE MOON
MUSIC FROM THE NETFLIX FILM

OVER
THE
MOON

© 2021 Maisie Music Publishing, LLC
NETFLIX and related artwork © 2020 Netflix, Inc. Used with permission.

ISBN 978-1-70515-710-7

HAL•LEONARD®

Visit Hal Leonard Online at
www.halleonard.com

Contact us:
Hal Leonard
7777 West Bluemound Road
Milwaukee, WI 53213
Email: info@halleonard.com

In Europe, contact:
Hal Leonard Europe Limited
42 Wigmore Street
Marylebone, London, W1U 2RN
Email: info@halleonardeurope.com

In Australia, contact:
Hal Leonard Australia Pty. Ltd.
4 Lentara Court
Cheltenham, Victoria, 3192 Australia
Email: info@halleonard.com.au

CONTENTS

ON THE MOON ABOVE

Words and Music by CHRISTOPHER CURTIS,
MARJORIE DUFFIELD and HELEN PARK

6

MOONCAKES

Words and Music by CHRISTOPHER CURTIS,
MARJORIE DUFFIELD and HELEN PARK

ROCKET TO THE MOON

Words and Music by CHRISTOPHER CURTIS,
MARJORIE DUFFIELD and HELEN PARK

ROCKET TO THE MOON
(Reprise)

Words and Music by CHRISTOPHER CURTIS,
MARJORIE DUFFIELD and HELEN PARK

ULTRALUMINARY

Words and Music by CHRISTOPHER CURTIS,
MARJORIE DUFFIELD and HELEN PARK

Slowly, freely

I'm the light ev-'ry night in your world. _____ Are you read-y to

watch _____ me be leg-en-dar-y? 'Cause I'm _____

Dance tempo

(Spoken:) ultra... luminary.

HEY BOY

Words and Music by CHRISTOPHER CURTIS,
MARJORIE DUFFIELD and HELEN PARK

WONDERFUL

Words and Music by CHRISTOPHER CURTIS,
MARJORIE DUFFIELD and HELEN PARK

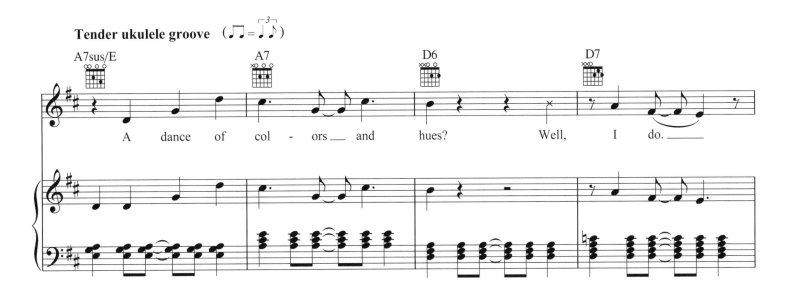

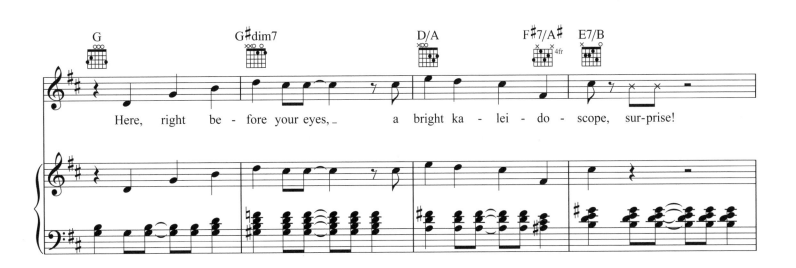

YOURS FOREVER

Words and Music by CHRISTOPHER CURTIS,
MARJORIE DUFFIELD and HELEN PARK

48

LOVE SOMEONE NEW

Words and Music by CHRISTOPHER CURTIS,
MARJORIE DUFFIELD and HELEN PARK

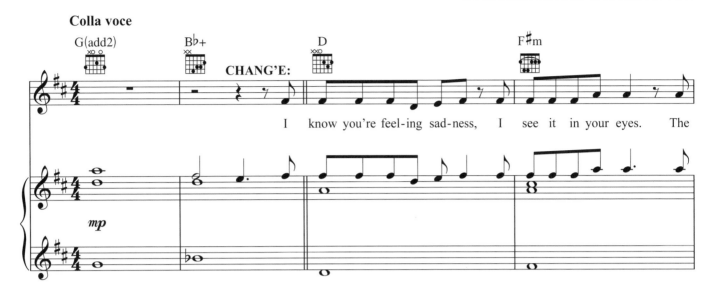

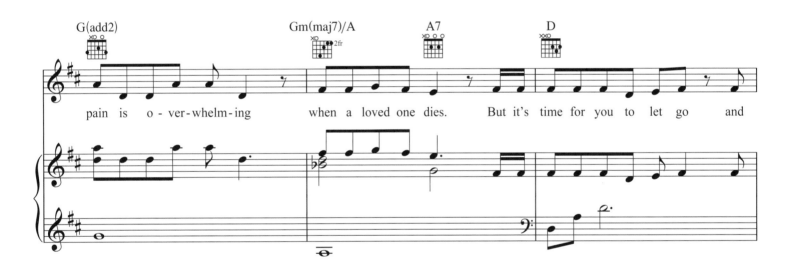